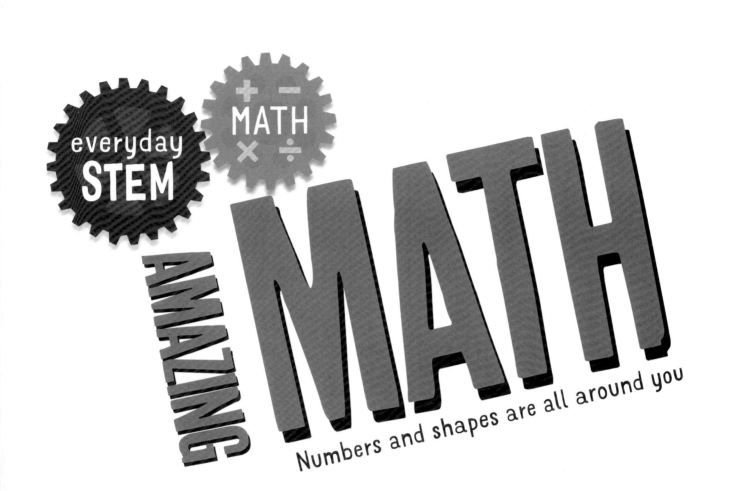

everyday STEM

MATH

AMAZING MATH

Numbers and shapes are all around you

KINGFISHER
LONDON & NEW YORK

First published 2022 in the United States by Kingfisher
120 Broadway, New York, NY 10271
Kingfisher is an imprint of Macmillan Children's Books, London
All rights reserved.

ISBN 978-0-7534-7842-4

Distributed in the U.S. and Canada by Macmillan,
120 Broadway, New York, NY 10271

Library of Congress Cataloging-in-Publication data has been applied for.

Author: Lou Abercrombie
Illustrator: Lilia Miceli
Series editor: Lizzie Davey
Series design: Jim Green

Kingfisher Books are available for special promotions and premiums.
For details contact:
Special Markets Department, Macmillan
120 Broadway, New York, NY 10271.

For more information please visit:
www.kingfisherbooks.com

Printed in China
2 4 6 8 9 7 5 3 1
1TR/0722/UG/WKT/128MA

EU representative: 1st Floor, The Liffey Trust Centre
117-126 Sheriff Street Upper, Dublin 1 D01 YC43

MIX
Paper from
responsible sources
FSC® C116313
FSC
www.fsc.org

CONTENTS

WHAT IS MATH?

Math is the science of numbers and shapes. It is the foundation of everything around us and everything we do. Thousands of years ago, many civilizations developed their own math, but it was the ancient Greeks who started looking at the world and wondering how it all connected. Out of this curiosity came logic, reasoning, and theories that could be applied to real-life problems. And presto—something useful was created!

The **buildings** around us have been designed, planned, and constructed using the measurements, angles, and calculations of geometry, trigonometry, arithmetic, and calculus.

Smartphones are the result of thousands of years of thinking! Factors are numbers another number can be divided by exactly—for example, 3 and 6 are factors of 12. They played a key part in the development of the theory of sound waves, which paved the way for the first antennae and eventually phones.

The **clothes** we wear are cloaked in math! Geometry can be found in their patterns, measurement in their designs, and arithmetic in the making process, where drawings need to be scaled up into life-size clothes. Even more arithmetic and problem-solving is used on the business end for budgeting, selling, and marketing the finished items.

HYPATIA OF ALEXANDRIA (A.D. 355-415)

The Mother of Math was taught by her father, who was considered one of the most educated men in Alexandria. She studied everything! Arts, literature, science, philosophy, and physical education, which included rowing, swimming, and horse riding. But it was math Hypatia had a true talent for. She was a wise woman, prominent thinker, and a great teacher. Widely admired, she is often held up as an icon for women's rights. Going against the norm of what was expected, Hypatia dressed and behaved differently, often riding around freely in her own chariot.

Cars are powered by math. Thousands of calculations, equations, and formulas have gone into ensuring their performance, comfort, and safety. Car design uses geometry and measurement. Ratios are used in engines, and numbers indicate speed, license plates, tire size, and so on.

DID YOU KNOW?

The word "mathematics" comes from the ancient Greek word "máthēma," which means "that which is learned" or "what one gets to know." Math has many branches, including arithmetic, geometry, and calculus. It can be roughly split into pure math (theory) and applied math (application), though many things in our everyday lives are a result of both.

TYPES OF NUMBERS

A world without numbers would be very strange! How would you know your age or your birthday? How would you bake without ingredient quantities? How would you shop without knowing something's value? And how would you get in touch with anyone without telephone numbers and addresses? Numbers are useful for all of these things. There are many types of numbers, and they can be grouped together into different categories.

DID YOU KNOW?

The square of odd numbers is odd, while the square of even numbers is always even!

NATURAL NUMBERS

These are whole numbers such as 1, 2, 3, 4, 5, 6, 7, 8, 9, and 10. Zero is not a natural number.

WHOLE NUMBERS

The numbers we count with every day are known as whole numbers—for example, 0, 1, 2, 3, 4, and 5.

INTEGERS

Integers include whole numbers and their negative mirror images, with zero in the middle—for example, −2, −1, 0, 1, and 2. Integers stretch all the way to infinity in both directions.

PRIME NUMBERS

These are numbers that can only be divided by one and themselves. The first five prime numbers are 2, 3, 5, 7, and 11. Prime numbers are essential in modern computer technology.

LEARNING WITH NUMBERS

We learn number facts to help us with the arithmetic we use in our everyday lives. Here are a few examples:

- Times tables
- Square numbers—numbers that are multiplied by themselves, such as 2 x 2 = 4, 3 x 3 = 9, and 4 x 4 = 16.
- Even numbers can always be divided by two.
- Odd numbers can't be divided by two without leaving a remainder.

$$2 \times 2 = 4$$
$$3 \times 3 = 9$$
$$4 \times 4 = 16$$

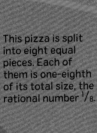

This pizza is split into eight equal pieces. Each of them is one-eighth of its total size, the rational number $\frac{1}{8}$.

RATIONAL NUMBERS

These are numbers that can be expressed as the ratio of two integers. They include whole numbers, fractions, and exact decimals—decimals that can be written as fractions; for example, $0.33333\ldots = \frac{1}{3}$.

IRRATIONAL NUMBERS

Numbers that can't be written as a ratio or fraction. For example, the square root of 2 is a decimal with an infinite number of digits: $1.41421356237\ldots$

SRINIVASA RAMANUJAN (1887-1920)

Srinivasa Ramanujan was a self-taught Indian mathematician who loved number theory and formulas. As a child he was obstinate. He barely talked at age three and hated school at age five. However, by 11 he was excelling in math. At 15 Ramanujan borrowed a library book containing 5,000 mathematical theorems. He set himself the challenge of writing a formula for each theorem. Ramanujan died at only 33 years old, but he left behind three notebooks and a few scraps of paper detailing 3,900 formulas. Over 100 years later, scientists and scholars are still using his formulas for their research.

NUMERALS AND NUMBERS

The idea of a number can be expressed in different ways. For example, you can express the idea of three by clapping your hands three times, by holding up three fingers, by saying the word three, or by writing down the symbol 3. The number system we use today was created over 1,500 years ago by Indian and Arabic mathematicians. It uses numerals made up of the digits 0, 1, 2, 3, 4, 5, 6, 7, 8, and 9. It is a decimal system—the place value of each digit in a numeral represents a multiple of ten.

DID YOU KNOW?

The word "hundred" comes from the old Norse word "hundrath," which means 120, not 100!

WHAT IS A NUMERAL?

Numerals are the symbols or names we use to show numbers. 13, 1, and 12 are all numerals. Look around and you will see them everywhere. We use numerals as labels to help us identify things, such as which house is which.

PARKING LOT MATH PROBLEM

This popular puzzle is about figuring out which parking space numeral the car is covering up. But the main question to ask yourself is how are the numbers being used here?

Answer: The numbers are upside down—the missing number is 87.

NUMEROLOGY

The study of numbers and finding meaning in them is called numerology. Numbers are often considered to be lucky or unlucky, depending on where in the world you are.

LUCKY:
US, UK, France, Netherlands

7

UNLUCKY:
China, Vietnam, Thailand

LUCKY:
Italy

13

UNLUCKY:
US, UK, Sweden

LUCKY:
Germany

4

UNLUCKY:
Japan, China

LUCKY:
China, Vietnam, Japan

8

UNLUCKY:
India

WHAT IS A NUMBER?

Numbers are an essential part of our everyday lives. They are expressed in words or symbols and represent the idea of a particular amount. When we read a number, we consider each digit and its place value. For example, the number 215 is read as "two hundred fifteen" and is made up of the digits 2, 1, and 5. Here are a few of the ways we use numbers:

Telling the time

Counting and quantifying

Comparing and ordering

Calculating

9

NEGATIVE NUMBERS

Negative numbers are the real numbers found to the left of zero on a number line. They can be hard to understand—because how can you have less than nothing? However, negative numbers are often very useful, because there are plenty of times when things are less than zero. It depends on how they are measured and where we have decided to put zero in the first place!

ACCOUNTING

On bank statements, negative numbers are used to show money going out of our accounts (what we have spent) and debt (when we have spent more than we have).

```
-  4.20
-  16
-  21
-  3.50
-  2.25
─────────
-46.95
─────────
```

ECONOMY

Negative numbers are used to show when companies have made a loss and when an economy has declined. If the economy declines for more than a few months at a time—expressed by negative numbers—this is called a recession. In the 1980s, the United States experienced a double-dip recession, which means it had back-to-back periods when its economy shrank, with periods of positive growth in between.

DID YOU KNOW?

Negative numbers were first used in China, in 200 B.C. Many civilizations were reluctant to use them. The ancient Egyptians thought negative numbers were ridiculous, because their math was based on measurement.

FAHRENHEIT [°F]

120
100
80
60
40
20
0
-20
-40

CELSIUS [°C]

50
40
30
20
10
0
-10
-20
-30
-40

TEMPERATURE

Negative numbers are used to show when temperatures are below 0. Water freezes at 32°F, which is 0°C.

BUILDINGS

Negative numbers are used to show building levels that are below the first floor. Some buildings even have multiple basement levels, which can be labeled as −1, −2, −3, and so on.

FLOOR 3

FLOOR 2

FLOOR 1

BASEMENT −1

USING NUMBERS

Numbers are ingrained in our daily lives. We phone family, shop with friends, celebrate birthdays, and play games. Whether it's numerals or numbers, basic arithmetic or small calculations, math and numbers are such a natural part of our world that most people don't even realize they're using them! Every job in the world uses numbers in some form— here are a few examples.

THE MATH OF BALLET

How do ballerinas use math? They use numbers when counting along to dance in time with the music, and to understand what 1st, 2nd, 3rd, 4th, and 5th positions are. Mathematical problem-solving helps them determine how much force to put into a pirouette, turn, or leap, and how to balance en pointe. Geometry is needed to understand the angles of the body and to use symmetry and asymmetry to tell a story.

A MOUTHFUL OF NUMBERS

Dentists use math too! Our teeth are given numbers so that dentists can accurately record details about each individual tooth. Arithmetic is used to carefully calculate the correct dose of an anaesthetic. Teeth are measured before any root canal work is undertaken. When fitting crowns, dentists measure the existing tooth in order to calculate how much of it needs to be ground down before the crown is fitted.

IN THE CLASSROOM

Teachers use math and numbers all the time. They count students when they call the roll. Grading homework and tests means using fractions and percentages. Also, there is math in all of the teaching subjects, from the obvious math and science to English, poetry, music, and art.

$1 \times 4 = 4$
$2 \times 4 = 8$
$3 \times 4 = 12$
$4 \times 4 = 16$
$5 \times 4 = 20$
$6 \times 4 = 24$

MARJORIE LEE BROWNE (1914–1979)

Marjorie Lee Browne was a mathematician and teacher. She was one of the first African-American women to gain a PhD in mathematics. Browne believed in math education for everyone and could see the importance of early learning to promote confidence. She taught and inspired teachers, and her immense enthusiasm helped improve the quality of math education in North Carolina. Browne loved pure math, describing a mathematician as someone who "appreciates the beauty, power, and eloquence of mathematics as one of the greatest art forms."

IF I HAD TO DO MY LIFE AGAIN, I WOULDN'T DO ANYTHING ELSE. I LOVE MATH!

EVERYDAY FRACTIONS AND DECIMALS

In the real world, the numbers we use aren't always whole. In fact, we regularly need to work with parts of things when dealing with quantities and proportions. In measurement and scale, there is often a need for more precision than whole numbers can give us. This is where fractions and decimals come in. They're an essential math skill that we use throughout our daily lives.

FRACTIONS

There are three types of fractions. They are written as numbers stacked on top of each other, divided by a line.

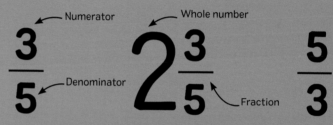

PROPER FRACTIONS

These have a numerator that is smaller than their denominator.

MIXED FRACTIONS

In mixed fractions, whole numbers and fractions are combined. The whole numbers are written first.

IMPROPER FRACTIONS

Here the numerator is bigger than the denominator—the fraction is bigger than a whole.

TIME

We use fractions every second, minute, and hour of the day!

1 second = $\frac{1}{60}$ of a minute

1 minute = $\frac{1}{60}$ of an hour

1 hour = $\frac{1}{24}$ of a day

1 day = $\frac{1}{7}$ of a week

DID YOU KNOW?

The ancient Egyptians only used unit fractions, which means their numerator was always one. Instead of writing $\frac{2}{3}$ they would write $\frac{1}{2} + \frac{1}{6}$.

BAKING

In recipes, ingredients are written using whole numbers and fractions. Imagine how disgusting something might taste without fractions!

WOW, THAT'S SALTY!

TESTS AND EXAMS

When you take a test, you are sometimes given a score that is based on the number of answers you got right, compared with the total number of questions—that's a fraction.

DECIMALS

Decimals are another way of showing parts of numbers. We use them every day—here are three examples of how.

1.2

Parts of numbers are shown to the right of the decimal point.

Decimal point

Whole numbers are shown to the left of the decimal point.

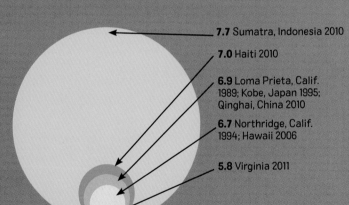

7.7 Sumatra, Indonesia 2010

7.0 Haiti 2010

6.9 Loma Prieta, Calif. 1989; Kobe, Japan 1995; Qinghai, China 2010

6.7 Northridge, Calif. 1994; Hawaii 2006

5.8 Virginia 2011

EARTHQUAKES

The Moment Magnitude Scale (MMS) tells us the size of an earthquake. Scientists measure the amount of movement and energy an earthquake releases, then convert it into a decimal number, which allows us to compare it to other earthquakes. MMS is a logarithmic scale, which means that for each whole number it goes up, the magnitude is ten times bigger.

MONEY

Currency is expressed in decimals. For example, a dollar, pound, or euro is the whole amount and is written to the left of the decimal point. Cents and pence are not whole numbers and are written to the right, to two decimal places. For example: $1.72.

HEALTH

Decimals are used when calculating a person's health risk using scales such as BMI (body mass index) and WHR (waist-to-hip ratio). They take into account a person's weight and height, as well as other factors such as muscle density, body shape, eating habits, and activity levels.

SHOPPING WITH MATH

Imagine arranging to meet some friends. You will have a day out shopping and have lunch together. It's hard to believe that fractions and decimals play any part in this, but they do! Math is in everything, including counting your money, figuring out your travel plans, and sticking to a budget when you spend.

BUDGETING

You can't go shopping without knowing how much money you have. You will also need to think about whether you have enough to buy what you want to. Don't forget to include money for travel and snacks!

SCHEDULING

Trying to meet someone at a certain time isn't as easy as you think. You will need to consider:

- When and where are you meeting?
- Do you need to go by train or bus, or can you walk?
- How long does it take to get there?
- How long will you be out, and how will you get home?

To make it easier to estimate travel times, we work in fractions of hours and round up. For a 25-minute bus ride, allow half an hour. For a 10-minute walk, allow a quarter of an hour.

DID YOU KNOW?

Reducing the cost of something by reducing the left digit by one is known as charm pricing. Your brain processes $10 and $9.99 as two different things, despite them only being a penny different.

SPLITTING THE BILL

Unless you have a very generous friend, you'll need to divide up the check. That means using fractions and decimals again.

SHOPPING

Shopping with friends is a lot of fun, but it's easy to get carried away and spend too much. It's best to work to a budget and keep track of what you've spent. If you budget in your head, it's easier to work with whole dollars and round up or down so that you can do the addition more easily.

SHARING A PIZZA

All that shopping can make you hungry, but you've spent so much you only have enough for one pizza. How do you make sure it's shared fairly? By slicing it into fractions, of course!

THE NUMBERS BEHIND A PHOTO

Photography is amazing! With the simple click of a button, the image that you see in front of you is reproduced on your camera as a digital file. It feels like magic, but there's actually a whole lot of math going on inside your camera, involving whole numbers, fractions, and decimals, not to mention the calculations and measurements that the photographer has to consider.

FOCAL LENGTH

Photographers use different lenses with different focal lengths depending on their distance from and type of subject. For example, a wide-angle lens is used for landscape photography, while a telephoto lens is used for sports.

IT'S FORMULAIC

Photographers use a basic formula when choosing their camera settings:

Exposure is proportional to aperture x shutter speed x ISO sensitivity

ISO controls brightness. ISO 100 is used for bright conditions, and ISO 1600 for dark.

INSIDE A CAMERA

Light rays

A photographer's job is to control how much light enters their camera. Cameras are designed to allow them to do this very precisely—here's a simplified look at what's inside.

The **aperture** controls how much light enters the camera.

APERTURE

The amount of light that enters a camera is expressed in simple decimals:

f/2.8 = 1/2.8 = 0.35714286
f/5.6 = 1/5.6 = 0.17857143

The smaller the f-stop number, the larger the camera's opening, which means that more light is let in.

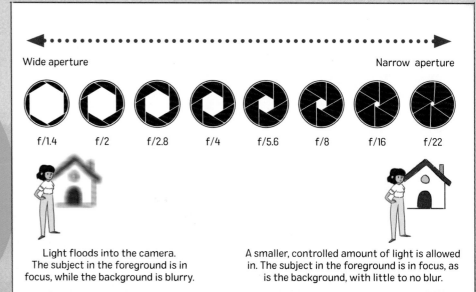

Wide aperture   Narrow aperture

f/1.4   f/2   f/2.8   f/4   f/5.6   f/8   f/16   f/22

Light floods into the camera. The subject in the foreground is in focus, while the background is blurry.

A smaller, controlled amount of light is allowed in. The subject in the foreground is in focus, as is the background, with little to no blur.

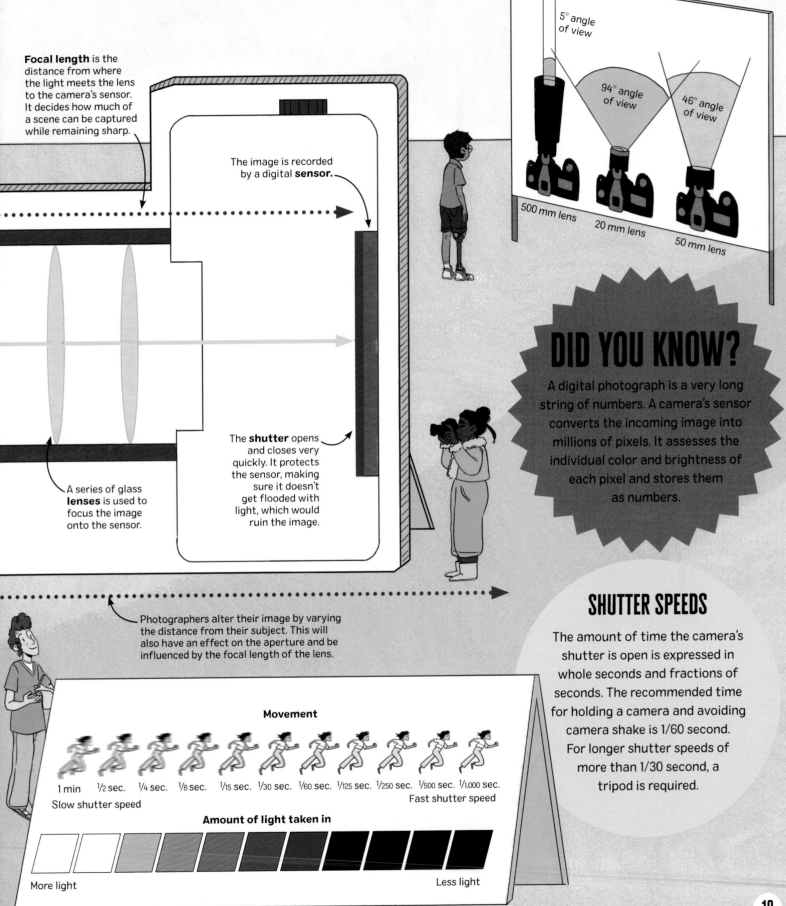

Focal length is the distance from where the light meets the lens to the camera's sensor. It decides how much of a scene can be captured while remaining sharp.

The image is recorded by a digital **sensor.**

A series of glass **lenses** is used to focus the image onto the sensor.

The **shutter** opens and closes very quickly. It protects the sensor, making sure it doesn't get flooded with light, which would ruin the image.

5° angle of view

94° angle of view

46° angle of view

500 mm lens

20 mm lens

50 mm lens

DID YOU KNOW?

A digital photograph is a very long string of numbers. A camera's sensor converts the incoming image into millions of pixels. It assesses the individual color and brightness of each pixel and stores them as numbers.

Photographers alter their image by varying the distance from their subject. This will also have an effect on the aperture and be influenced by the focal length of the lens.

SHUTTER SPEEDS

The amount of time the camera's shutter is open is expressed in whole seconds and fractions of seconds. The recommended time for holding a camera and avoiding camera shake is 1/60 second. For longer shutter speeds of more than 1/30 second, a tripod is required.

Movement

1 min   1/2 sec.   1/4 sec.   1/8 sec.   1/15 sec.   1/30 sec.   1/60 sec.   1/125 sec.   1/250 sec.   1/500 sec.   1/1,000 sec.

Slow shutter speed

Fast shutter speed

Amount of light taken in

More light

Less light

BUILDING WITH MATH

Have you ever thought about the math that has gone into putting a roof over your head? The homes we live in are built with arithmetic, fractions, and decimals. Planning a building requires an architect's drawings and an engineer's calculations. In the budgeting phase, building contractors use measurements to determine the cost of material and manpower required. And then, of course, there's the construction itself!

A **construction manager** manages the different contractors. They order materials and oversee the budget, using a combination of fractions and decimals.

Builders work closely with the architect's drawings and engineer's measurements. They do their own calculations and measurements, which use decimals because they need to be very precise.

DID YOU KNOW?

The tallest tower ever made with wooden toy blocks was built in Lyon, France, in 2016. The completed structure used 9,834 wooden planks, took 16 hours to build, and stood 60.4 ft. (18.4 m) high.

Electricians use fractions and decimals to determine room dimensions and wiring lengths. They convert watts to kilowatts and calculate electrical load to figure out which fuses are needed.

Electricians use Ohm's law to determine what voltage is running through an electrical circuit:

Voltage = Current x Resistance

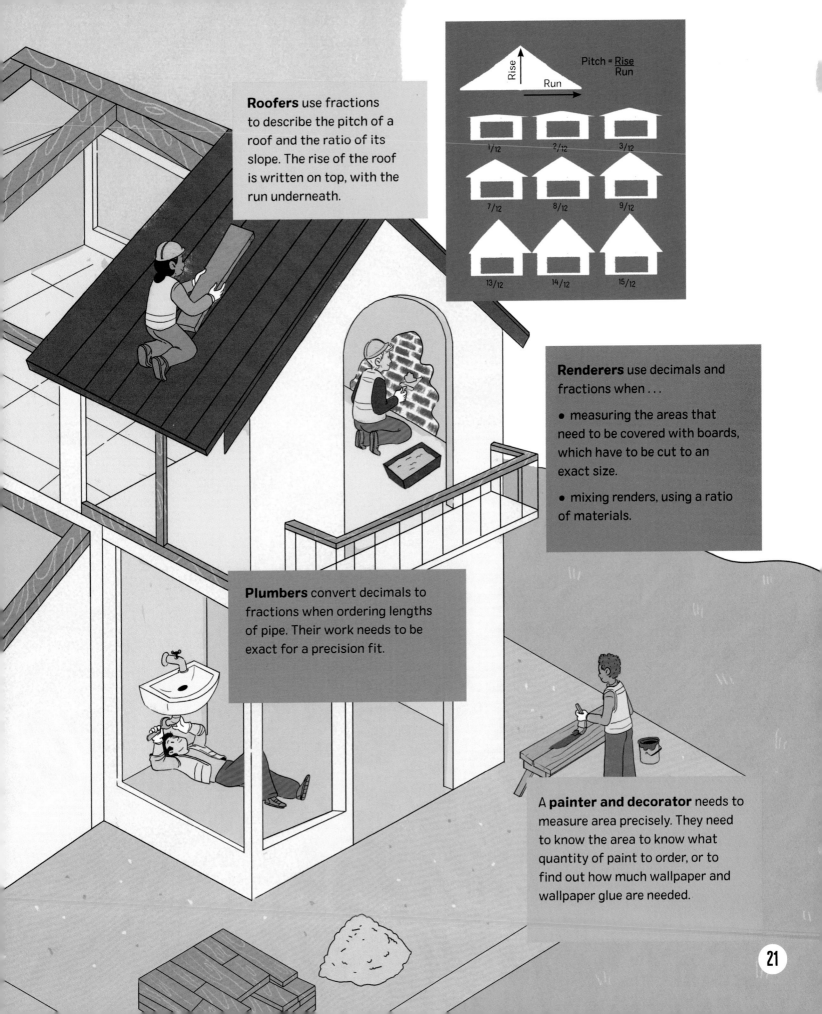

Roofers use fractions to describe the pitch of a roof and the ratio of its slope. The rise of the roof is written on top, with the run underneath.

Pitch = $\frac{\text{Rise}}{\text{Run}}$

Rise

Run

1/12 2/12 3/12

7/12 8/12 9/12

13/12 14/12 15/12

Renderers use decimals and fractions when . . .

• measuring the areas that need to be covered with boards, which have to be cut to an exact size.

• mixing renders, using a ratio of materials.

Plumbers convert decimals to fractions when ordering lengths of pipe. Their work needs to be exact for a precision fit.

A **painter and decorator** needs to measure area precisely. They need to know the area to know what quantity of paint to order, or to find out how much wallpaper and wallpaper glue are needed.

21

THE STORY OF A CIRCLE

Circles are everywhere. They are in everyday objects such as cars and bikes, plates and glasses, coins, jewelry, and clocks. An important element of circle design is their dimensions, including circumference and diameter. This is where the irrational number pi (π) comes in. People have been trying to determine an accurate value for pi for over 4,000 years. The ancient Babylonians figured it at 3.125, while the ancient Egyptians said 3.16. Then the ancient Greek mathematician Archimedes came along. His number was more accurate and was based on mathematical theory instead of measurement.

CIRCLE FORMULAS

Circumference of a circle = $2\pi r$

Area of a circle = πr^2 ← radius

Volume of a cylinder = $\pi r^2 h$ ← height

Area of a sphere = $4\pi r^2$

Volume of a sphere = $\frac{4}{3}\pi r^3$

ARCHIMEDES
(c. 287–212 b.c.)

As an astronomer, engineer, inventor, mathematician, and physicist, Archimedes was probably the greatest scientist of his time. Like other ancient Greek mathematicians, he was interested in the theory of how things worked. His method for measuring pi involved drawing polygons inside and outside a circle. He made observations about the perimeters of the polygons and how they related to pi. Archimedes went from a hexagon to a 12-sided polygon, and kept on doubling the number of sides until he had a 96-sided polygon! His final estimate for pi was between 3.1408 and 3.1428, which is accurate to two decimal places.

SPORTS

Circles and spheres are used throughout the world of sports. A center spot marks the center point of a soccer field. Ice hockey players must have entered a semi-circle in front of the goal before scoring. Then there's the circular launch area that defines the movement of a shot putter. Plus, of course, there's the spherical shape of all the balls!

Tennis balls are brightly colored and designed to bounce.

Soccer balls are round but are often patterned with a series of pentagons and hexagons.

Ice hockey uses a puck—a cylinder with two circular faces.

Shots are small but very heavy balls—they are made of solid metal.

Basketball hoops are circular, with space for the ball to drop through them.

THE BIGGEST BALL

Here are the diameters of some of the balls you are most likely to come across.

Table tennis
1.6 in. (4 cm)

Golf
1.7 in. (4.3 cm)

Tennis
2.6 in. (6.7 cm)

Baseball
2.86 in. (7.2 cm)

Shot
4.7 in. (12 cm)

Soccer
8.7 in. (22 cm)

Basketball
9.5 in. (24.1 cm)

DID YOU KNOW?

The ancient Mesopotamian people are believed to have invented the wheel around 3200-4000 B.C. It's likely the wheel was also invented independently in China, around 2800 B.C. Either way, it's one of the most important inventions in human history!

NUMBERS IN NATURE

Number theory is the study of the properties and relationships between positive whole numbers such as 1, 2, 3, 4, and 5. Since ancient times, we have organized these natural numbers into different types—for example, odd, even, square, and prime numbers. One of the most fascinating relationships between numbers is the Fibonacci sequence, which can be related to the natural world around us.

THE FIBONACCI SEQUENCE

In this sequence, each number is the sum of the two numbers that come before it, starting with 0 and 1: 0, 1, 1, 2, 3, 5, 8, 13, 21, 34, and so on. It is one of the most famous formulas in mathematics, and first appeared in a book by Italian mathematician Fibonacci in 1202. The formula was originally conceived as the solution to a math problem about rabbits—it tried to keep track of rabbit numbers, with each male-female pair of rabbits having a male-female pair of babies every month.

one pair of young black rabbits

December

The black rabbits have become adults and can now reproduce.

January

February

The black rabbits have blue twins.

The black rabbits have red twins.

March

The black rabbits have brown twins.

The red rabbits have green twins.

April

May

The blue rabbits have gray twins.

The black rabbits have pink twins.

The red rabbits have orange twins.

DID YOU KNOW?

The golden ratio isn't actually a ratio—it's an irrational number!

THE GOLDEN RATIO

The golden ratio is a number, 1.618 . . . , which is often found in nature. Things with proportions that match the ratio often appear beautiful to us, and people are naturally drawn to them. The Fibonacci sequence is closely linked to the golden ratio. If you divide a number from the sequence by its predecessor, the result becomes closer to the golden ratio as the sequence moves closer to infinity.

$$\frac{3}{2} = 1.5, \quad \frac{5}{3} = 1.667, \quad \frac{8}{5} = 1.6$$

THE FAMILY TREE OF A HONEYBEE

The rabbit problem is only a theory—rabbits don't actually breed that way. However, there are other examples where the Fibonacci sequence numbers do work. Every beehive has a female queen bee that lays the eggs. If an egg isn't fertilized, it produces a male honeybee. If an egg is fertilized, it produces a female honeybee. When we look at the ancestry of a male bee, we can see the Fibonacci sequence in action.

Generation
1
2
3
4
5
6

Number of bees
1
1
2
3
5
8

Male = 🐝   Queen = 🐝

Sunflower

THE GOLDEN SPIRAL

The golden spiral is a spiral in which the size of the curve increases in accordance with the Fibonacci sequence numbers. It can be found throughout nature, in pineapples, snail shells, seashells, sunflowers, pine cones, and succulent plants.

Succulent plant

Shell

25

EVERYDAY SUMS

Our word "arithmetic" comes from a Greek word, "arithmos," meaning "number." It means the study of numbers and how we can manipulate them to solve problems—for example, using the four basic operations: addition, subtraction, multiplication, and division. Arithmetic is the type of math that we use most often in our everyday lives.

Addition is the process of finding the total of two or more numbers.

2 + 1 = 3

3 − 1 = 2

Subtraction is the opposite of addition— where we take one or more numbers away from another number.

2 x 2 = 4

Multiplication is the process of adding a set of numbers together a certain amount of times. We can also scale something up this way.

4 ÷ 2 = 2

Division is the opposite of multiplication. It is the way we split up something into equal parts.

Exponentiation is the repeated multiplication of a number with itself. It's shown as a power. So five to the power of three is 5^3, which means 5 x 5 x 5. The small number here is called an index.

ARITHMETIC FACTS

- Changing the order of the numbers in an addition problem doesn't change the answer, but in a subtraction problem it does!

- Most math symbols were created in the 1500s. Before that, problems were written out as words.

UNSOLVED

The Goldbach conjecture is one of the world's most famous unsolved math problems and has been around for 257 years. It states that every even number greater than 2 is the sum of two prime numbers—for example 2 + 2 = 4, 3 + 3 = 6, 7 + 13 = 20. However, because the sequence of numbers is infinite, no one has been able to definitively prove the theory.

ORDER OF OPERATIONS

Math problems are read from left to right. The different parts of the problem must be done in a set order to get the correct answer:

1. Grouped symbols such as those inside brackets

2. Indexes (exponentiation)

3. Division and multiplication

4. Addition and subtraction

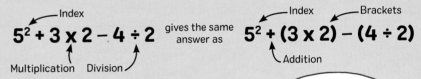

$$5^2 + 3 \times 2 - 4 \div 2 \quad \text{gives the same answer as} \quad 5^2 + (3 \times 2) - (4 \div 2)$$

Index — 5^2; Multiplication — 3×2; Division — $4 \div 2$; Index — 5^2; Brackets — (3×2); Addition — $(4 \div 2)$

MUHAMMAD AL-KHWARIZMI (780–850)

In the 800s, there was a great library in Baghdad, in what is now Iraq. It attracted many scholars, including the Persian mathematician Muhammad Al-Khwarizmi. There he was encouraged to write a book about calculation, which aimed to help readers with useful everyday math. In his Al-jabr section he produced step-by-step methods for solving equations quickly. These steps later became well known—as algebra.

WHEN I CONSIDER WHAT PEOPLE GENERALLY WANT IN CALCULATING, I FIND THAT IT ALWAYS IS A NUMBER.

HOW TO PARTY WITH MATH

Have you ever thought about the amount of arithmetic that has gone into a birthday party? There's picking a date, writing your guest list, finding a venue, and planning how much food is required. All that planning requires math. But what about the actual party? The table plans, the gifts, the dancing—you use math then too.

Picking a date: setting a date and picking a venue means checking your calendar and figuring out dates and timings. How far in advance is it? How long is the party going to be? Plenty of counting is required to work everything out.

The guest list: how many people can fit in your venue? How many are on the list? Do the totals match, or do you need to take off a few names? How many invitations do you need? When do you want a response by? Counting and calculation are needed to find the answers to these questions.

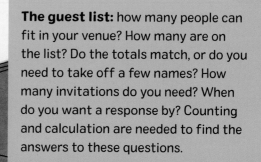

Party food: once you know your guest numbers, you will need to use multiplication to determine how much party food you will need. How many sandwiches do you need to make so that each guest can have two? What about veggies, chips, and fruit skewers? Then there's the cake! How big does it need to be for everyone to get a generous slice?

Dancing: have you ever realized that you're doing math when you're dancing at a party? Unless you're dancing really badly, you will be subconsciously counting out the beat and dancing along in time to it.

Gifts: guests need to use math too. Wrapping a present requires measuring the gift and cutting the correct amount of paper and ribbon to go around it.

DID YOU KNOW?

We have been having birthday parties since the first century, but the word "party" wasn't used until 1852. So it only took us 1852 – 100 = 1,752 years to catch on!

The seating plan: how many tables and chairs do you need? How do you decide who sits where? You'll need your division skills to figure this one out.

MATH AND THE INTERNET

Isn't it amazing what you can do on the Internet? You can search for anything and a multitude of answers will appear. You can text, email, chat, and see your friends on the other side of the world. You can even do all of this on small, handheld devices. It certainly doesn't feel like it has anything to do with math. However, computers and the Internet are entirely the result of numbers and equations.

COMPUTERS

Computers are the electronic devices we use to store and process data. Their physical parts, such as the central processing unit, mouse, keyboard, and monitor, are known as hardware. Software is the programming code that tells the computer what to do and how to do it.

The **Internet** is a worldwide computer network that runs on a complex set of rules, with data being moved from one place to another.

The brain of a computer is its **central processing unit** (CPU), which is made up of billions of tiny switches called transistors. The transistors are turned on and off by the flow of binary code.

BINARY CODE

Binary code is based on the binary number system, where 0 means off and 1 means on. The decimal number system we use day to day is a base 10 system, which means we count from 0 to 9 before we exchange for a 1. Binary is a base 2 number system, which means you count 0 and 1 before you exchange for a 1.

Base 10	Base 2
0	0
1	1
2	10
3	11
4	100
5	101
6	110
7	111
8	1000
9	1001
10	1010
11	1011

ALGORITHMS

Algorithms tell a computer how to execute a task or solve a problem. They work like strict instruction manuals, with a list of tasks that must be completed in a set order. The computer takes the input data, runs it through a step-by-step decision-making process of arithmetic, then transforms it into something new (the output). This is how a lot of the software we use works, including facial recognition software.

1. Input: scan face

2. Computation: Does it match?

Yes =
3. Output: allow access

No =
3. Output: refuse access

Software documents, music, and images are all stored in binary form. We use different **file formats** to help identify them, such as wav, jpeg, and ASCII.

USE YOUR HEAD!

A computer is fantastic for precise and fast data processing, but it isn't as powerful as the human brain. Our brains can undertake 38 quadrillion operations per second! Here are a few other comparisons:

COMPUTER

- Average storage: 1 TB (terabyte)
- Runs on: around 100W
- All information is treated the same

HUMAN BRAIN

- Estimated capacity: 1,000 TB
- Runs on: 10W, which makes it more energy efficient!
- Ability to prioritize memories based on importance

31

WHAT IS GEOMETRY?

Geometry is a branch of math that studies the size, shape, position, angles, and dimensions of things. It looks at the properties of points, lines, and surfaces, and the relationships between them. Squares, circles, and triangles are 2D shapes expressed in length and width, while cubes, spheres, and pyramids are 3D, with depth as the additional dimension. We can see all of these shapes in the world around us.

TYPES OF SHAPES

 A **polygon** is a 2D shape that has at least three straight sides and angles.

 A **polyhedron** is a 3D shape with a surface made up of polygons.

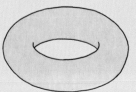 Unlike a polyhedron, a **curved 3D shape** has curves, and it can have holes in itself.

DID YOU KNOW?

The hardest 2D shape to draw is the circle. Our minds love the symmetry of circles, but our hands just can't do it!

MARYAM MIRZAKHANI (1977–2017)

Maryam Mirzakhani was born in Tehran, Iran, and grew up during the Iran-Iraq war. She was an avid reader who dreamed of becoming a writer.

To find the sum of all the integers from 1 to 100, split the numbers into two groups: 1–50 and 51–100.

1	2	3	4	5	. . .	49	50
100	99	98	97	96	. . .	52	51

Each pair can be added up to 101, and there are 50 pairs.

So the sum is 50 x 101 = 5,050

Mirzakhani's brother told her about a math problem involving adding up the integers from 1 to 100. She was fascinated by the beauty of its solution.

In 1994, Mirzakhani and her friend Roya Beheshti were the first girls ever to be part of the Iranian Mathematical Olympiad team.

After getting her undergraduate degree in math at Sharif University, Mirzakhani went to Harvard University, where she studied hyperbolic (curved) surfaces.

"IT'S SOOO COMPLICATED!"

Mirzakhani later worked at Princeton, and then at Stanford as a professor. Full of infectious excitement, she was known for her ability to play around with math theories and her willingness to pursue unsolvable problems.

She would often doodle complicated shapes on paper so that she could study their patterns.

"THE BEAUTY OF MATHEMATICS ONLY SHOWS ITSELF TO MORE PATIENT FOLLOWERS."

In 2014 Mirzakhani became the first woman and first Iranian to be awarded the Fields Medal, the highest honor in mathematics, for her contribution to the understanding of the symmetry of curved surfaces.

GEOMETRY IN NATURE

The word "geometry" comes from two Greek words—"geo," meaning earth, and "metria," to measure. It's easy to see why. The entire world can be classified as a sphere, and everything on it is in shape form. So much of nature is beautiful and pleasing to the eye. Why? Because of the natural occurrence of patterns, symmetry, and shape.

Reflective symmetry is where one side of a shape matches the other, across a central line.

SYMMETRY

In math, symmetry refers to an object that remains the same depending on how you transform it by translation, reflection, rotation, or scaling. In nature, objects that are symmetrical often seem to have well-balanced proportions.

Rotational symmetry is when you can rotate something around a central point and it continues to look the same.

DID YOU KNOW?

Spider webs have reflective and rotational symmetry. However, the degree of their symmetry depends on the spider's development —younger spiders construct more symmetrical webs.

SHAPE

Nature is full of 2D and 3D shapes, from the concentric circles made by a stone dropped in a pond to the perfect cubes of salt crystals. However, the most common shape in nature is the hexagon!

PATTERN

A fractal is a never-ending, repeated branching pattern. They can be found all over the place—for example, in how a river branches out, the shape of tree limbs, the blood vessels in your heart, and the forking of lightning bolts.

GEOMETRY IN BRIDGES

It's pretty jaw-dropping what engineers and architects can do. Take bridges, for example. They've been around for thousands of years, connecting societies, people, and places and overcoming obstacles of land and sea. As technology and engineering has developed, so have bridge designs. Many engineering advances occur thanks to precision calculations and our understanding of shapes and angles.

DID YOU KNOW?

The oldest datable bridge still in use is a slab-stone single arch over the Meles River in Izmir, Turkey. It dates back to 850 B.C.

The vertical **straight lines** of cable-stayed bridge towers transfer forces from the cables to the bridge's foundations.

SHAPES AND CALCULATIONS

Bridges come in all different shapes, sizes, and styles, but there are certain shapes, lines, and surfaces that crop up time after time.

The horizontal **straight line** of a bridge's platform gets us from A to B as quickly as possible.

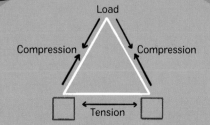

Load

Compression   Compression

Tension

Triangles are used in bridge building because they are a strong shape. As the weight of a load pushes down on the triangle, the compression it causes is spread across two sides of the triangle. This compression is then balanced out by the tension, or stretching, of the third side.

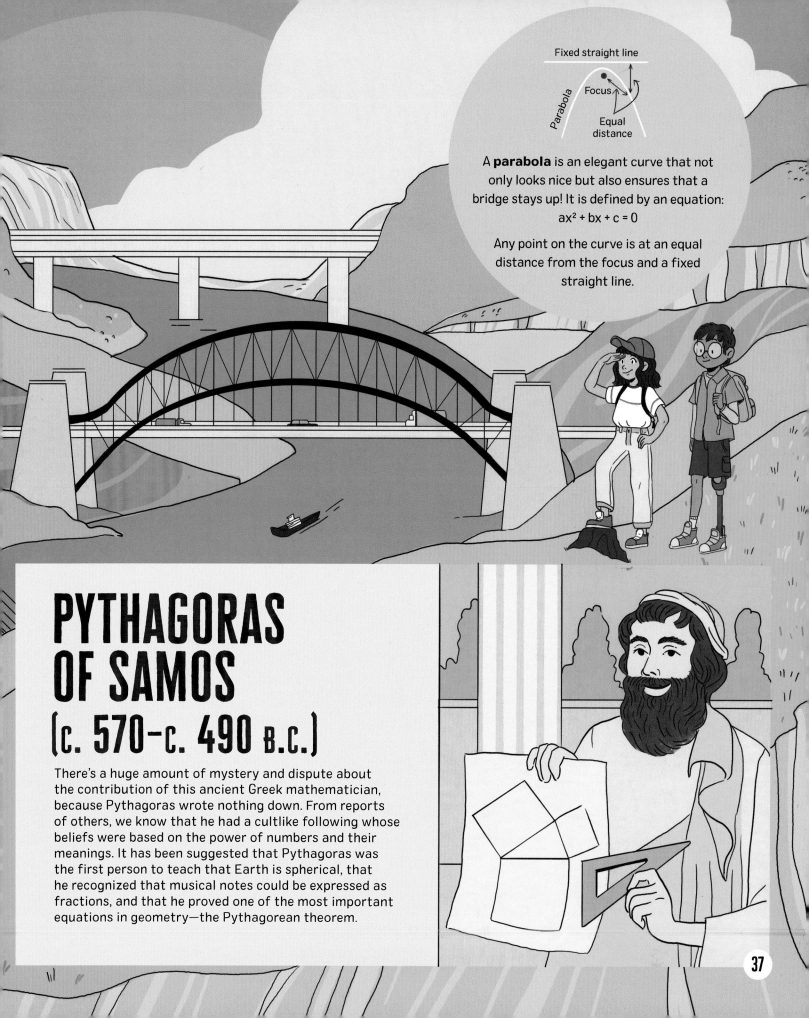

Fixed straight line

Focus

Parabola

Equal distance

A **parabola** is an elegant curve that not only looks nice but also ensures that a bridge stays up! It is defined by an equation: $ax^2 + bx + c = 0$

Any point on the curve is at an equal distance from the focus and a fixed straight line.

PYTHAGORAS OF SAMOS

(c. 570–c. 490 b.c.)

There's a huge amount of mystery and dispute about the contribution of this ancient Greek mathematician, because Pythagoras wrote nothing down. From reports of others, we know that he had a cultlike following whose beliefs were based on the power of numbers and their meanings. It has been suggested that Pythagoras was the first person to teach that Earth is spherical, that he recognized that musical notes could be expressed as fractions, and that he proved one of the most important equations in geometry—the Pythagorean theorem.

THE SHAPE OF FASHION DESIGN

The fashion industry is often thought of as one of the most creative, glamorous, and sought-after places to work, where artists are free to let their imaginations run wild. Surrounded by beautiful people jetting around the world and strutting down the catwalk in the latest must-have trends, there's not a number or calculation in sight! Or is there? Fashion is a fusion of business, science, art, and technology, and math is at its heart.

DESIGN IDEAS

Clothes designers use all kinds of geometry in their creations. They use the golden ratio, as well as other patterns and shapes. They must also have an understanding of how proportion works and how a 2D design will translate into three dimensions.

CUTTING A PATTERN

To convert a design into a dress pattern, designers scale up their drawings into life-size dimensions. This requires measurement skills, along with arithmetic and ratio.

CHOOSING MATERIALS

Designers must have a good knowledge of fabrics and an understanding of what they need out of them. How thick is the fabric? Does the design need to be warm, cool, thin, thick, stiff, or loose?

BUSINESS

Creating a cool design is one thing, but is it cost-effective? At the business end of fashion design, people figure out how to price items and make a profit. This requires arithmetic and percentages.

BUDGETING AND MAKING THE DESIGN

Arithmetic and critical math thinking are essential when . . .

• Figuring out how much fabric is needed, with an allowance for error.

• Understanding the widths of fabrics and how to determine what lengths are needed, depending on different widths.

• Using decimals and converting measurements from inches to yards.

GUIDED BY GEOMETRY

Humans are natural-born travelers. By land, sea, or air, we have been moving around the globe for a long time. And with Global Postioning System (GPS) technology, traveling is easier than ever. Have you ever considered how much math has gone into this technology? Geometry tells us about the angle and position of things. These two measurements are essential for navigating our way around the world.

LOST AT SEA

Imagine being stranded in the middle of the ocean with no land in sight and no GPS on hand. How would you know where you are?

Latitude is measured from the prime meridian, which runs through London.

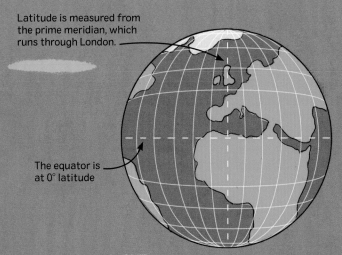

The equator is at 0° latitude

LATITUDE AND LONGITUDE

The globe can be divided into an imaginary grid. The horizontal lines running parallel to the equator are called latitude. They tell us how close to north or south we are. The vertical lines between the two poles are longitude and measure how far east or west a place is.

Latitude is calculated using a sextant, which measures the angle between the Sun and the horizon.

Longitude is calculated by measuring the local times in two places. For every 15 degrees we travel east, the local time increases by one hour. The opposite applies when traveling west.

A FLIGHT PATH OF NUMBERS

When does a pilot use geometry?

• For navigation—when planning routes, staying on course, and avoiding hazards.

• For safe takeoff—to ensure that the angle of ascent isn't too steep.

• For landing—pilots assess angle of descent using speed, altitude, and the distance from their destination.

DID YOU KNOW?

There are 31 active GPS satellites in orbit. Thanks to them, GPS can be found in many of our everyday devices, including cell phones, cars, and even our shoes!

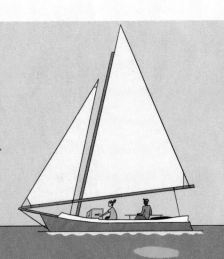

WHAT IS AN ANGLE?

An angle is the space formed when two lines meet at a shared point. Expressed in degrees, it measures the amount by which something has turned or rotated.

Angle

HOW GPS WORKS

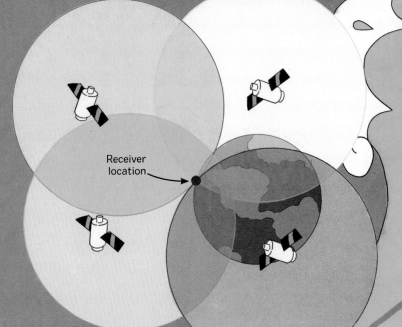

Receiver location

GPS uses a process called 3D trilateration. The receiver takes in signals from at least four different satellites, calculates its distance from them, and creates a sphere of possibility for each. The exact position of the receiver can then be determined by looking at the intersection of the spheres.

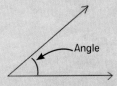

CALCULATOR MIND-READING TRICK

It's important to work on your mental arithmetic abilities, but it can also be fun to play with numbers on a calculator. When you get to the big numbers, math can even seem like magic!

YOU WILL NEED
- A calculator
- A willing victim
- A magician's hat for the full effect!

INSTRUCTIONS

1. Ask your victim to choose a three-digit number, then punch it into the calculator twice—for example, 234234.

2. Ask them to concentrate on the calculator's display, and act like you're using some incredible mind-reading skills.

3. Tell your victim that their number is divisible by 11, and ask them to verify by dividing it by 11.

4. Act cool when they gasp that you're right. Then keep the suspense building by telling them you're not finished.

5. Tell your victim that the result is also divisible by 13, and ask them to verify this.

6. Again, act cool when they gasp that you're right. Again, tell them that you're not done.

7. Get your victim to divide their result by their original three-digit number, such as 234.

8. Now's your chance to really pull out the magician act. Gaze knowingly into the middle distance, then tell them proudly that the final answer is 7.

CREATE A GOLDEN SPIRAL

A golden spiral spins out from a center point, with its curves crossing squares with sides the lengths of each term in the Fibonacci sequence. This experiment uses simple geometry to show you how to draw a golden spiral for yourself.

INSTRUCTIONS—START WITH SQUARES

1. Start by drawing two unit squares, one on top of the other. Each side of each square should be 1 unit long.

2. To the left of your first squares, draw a square with sides that are 2 units long.

3. Beneath all of these, draw a 3-unit square.

4. Draw a 5-unit square to the right of all of the squares you have drawn so far.

Each unit square has sides that are 1 unit long.

1

2

3

4

DRAW YOUR SPIRAL

1. Use your compass to draw quarter arcs between the corners of each square.

2. Start with the lower 1 unit square, and draw your arc from its bottom left to its top right.

3. Then use that top right point as the starting point for an arc in the other 1 unit square. You will be drawing from its bottom right to its top left.

4. Use the end of that arc as the starting point for your 2 unit square, and keep drawing arcs until you have one in every square. Your spiral is complete!

GET CREATIVE!
Why not color your spiral in? You could try turning it into something, such as a head. Or add another spiral and make it into a shell.

PLAYING WITH PI

Pi (π) is an irrational number that is used to calculate the dimensions of circles. Computer power means we now know it to 31 trillion decimal places, although most of the time 39 is more than enough! These two experiments will help you get to know pi.

CIRCUMFERENCE AND DIAMETER

1. Wrap your string around your dinner plate, then cut the string where the ends meet. This is your plate's circumference.

2. Take your cut length of string and stretch it across the widest part of the plate. Then cut the string to this length—this is your plate's diameter.

3. Repeat step 2 until all of your string is used up. You should find that you have three pieces of string plus a little bit. That's the value of pi!

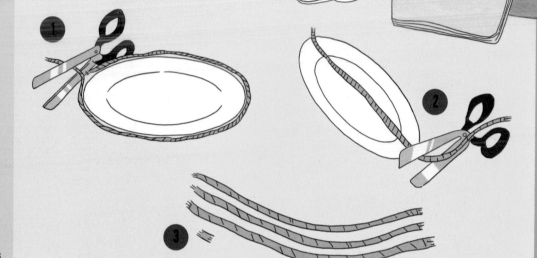

PI CITY

This city represents the digits of pi.

1. Draw a straight line across the bottom of your poster board. This will be the ground.

2. Starting on the left, draw blocks to represent each digit of pi. Each block will be 1 in. wide and a varying number of inches tall. The first digit is 3, so measure and draw a 3 in. x 1 in. rectangle.

3. Then draw a 1 in. tall rectangle, then 4 in., 1 in., and so on. Keep going until you have an up-and-down city skyline.

4. Color your city. You could add sky, windows, or even cars and people in the street below.

π = 3.14159265350897932384 6

BUILD THE PYTHAGOREAN THEOREM

The Pythagorean theorem states that the squares of the two shorter sides of a right triangle (a triangle with a right angle) add up to the same size as the square of its longest side. We can prove it by building squares for each side.

YOU WILL NEED
- Building bricks in three different colors

YOUR TURN!

INSTRUCTIONS

First, choose some numbers to work with: 3, 4, and 5 work well, or you could double them and try 6, 8, and 10.

1. Use your bricks to make a right triangle. Use a different color for each side, and make each side the length of one of the numbers you chose above.

2. Then use your bricks to turn each side into a square, with four sides of the same length. Does it look like the two smaller squares add up to the same as the bigger one? It's hard to imagine, so let's prove they're the same.

This side is 8 units long

This side is 6 units long

This side is 10 units long. It is the longest side, the hypotenuse, and is opposite the right angle of the triangle.

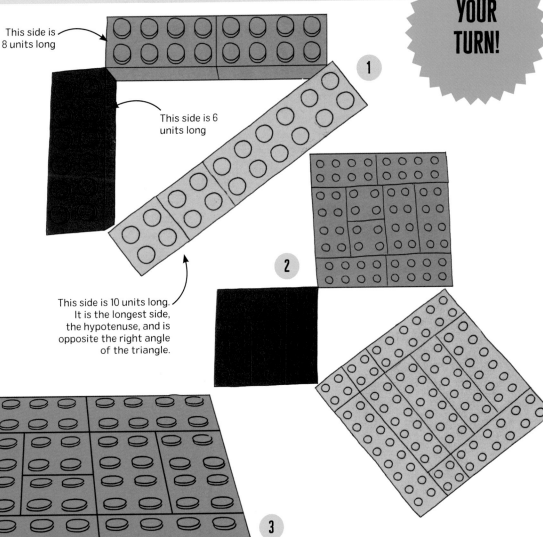

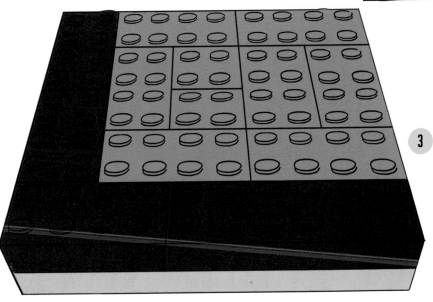

3. Transfer the bricks from the two smaller squares onto the top of the biggest square. You should find that there are no bricks left in the two smaller squares, and the biggest square has been completely covered.

GLOSSARY

Anesthetic
A type of medicine that puts people to sleep or stops them from feeling pain.

Antenna
A metal structure made to send or receive radio waves.

Architect
A person who designs buildings and gives advice about how they should be constructed.

Asymmetry
Lack of symmetry.

Budgeting
Planning how much you will spend on something or how much money something will make.

Engineer
A person who uses math and science to solve problems and to create machines and structures—for example, to make sure buildings are constructed properly, safely, and in the right place.

En pointe
Pronounced "on point"—the term used to describe ballet dancers dancing on the tips of their toes.

Infinity
The idea of something that goes on for ever. It is an idea rather than a number. It is written with this symbol: ∞

Intersection
A point or line where something crosses over with something else.

Logic
A way of solving problems based on careful thought and reasoning.

Mesopotamia
A region of southwest Asia where the world's earliest civilizations began (the area includes modern-day Syria, Turkey, and Iraq).

Percentage
Expressed in parts per hundred. For example, 25 percent means 25 out of every 100. It can also be written as ¼ or 0.25. If you got a score of 5 out of 20 on a test, that could also be expressed as 25 percent.

Philosophy
The study of some of the big questions about life and what it means to be human.

Pirouette
The word for a particular kind of spinning movement in dance.

Pixel
A tiny dot of light that makes up an image on a computer screen.

Profit
Money made by a person or company, not counting how much they have spent.

Theorem
A mathematical idea that has been proved.

Picture credits

The Publisher would like to thank the following for permission to reproduce their material.

Top = t; Bottom = b; Center = c; Left = l; Right = r

11 theasis/iStock Images; 23b Mochipet/Shutterstock; 25l UrsaHoogle/iStock Images, 25c Sabine Hortebusch/iStock Images, 25r mtreasure/iStock Images; 34tl Michael Burrell, 34tc malerapaso/iStock Images, 34tr vidok/iStock Images, 34bl Savany/iStock Images, 34bc assaive/iStock Images, 34br Alexander Bashkirov/iStock Images; 35tl sufiyan huseen/iStock Images, 35tr florintt/iStock Images, 35c Jennifer_Sharp/iStock Images, 35l hraun/iStock Images, 35bc SeanXu/iStock Images, 35br jerbarber/iStock Image; parking lot puzzle on page 6 reproduced with kind permission from David J. Bodycombe.

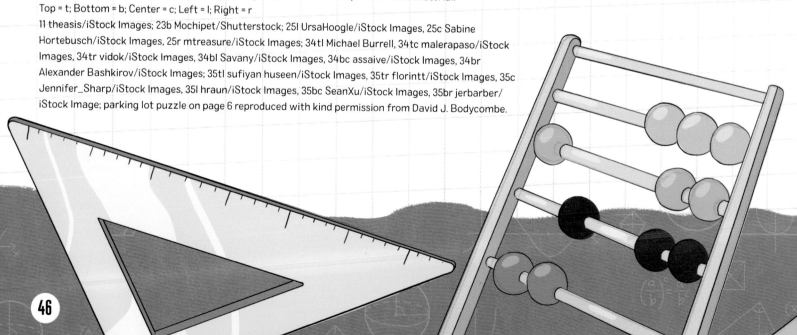

INDEX

THE AUTHOR & ILLUSTRATOR

LOU ABERCROMBIE

Lou has always loved numbers. She studied at Durham University in England, where she gained a first class bachelor of science degree in mathematics. She now writes fiction and nonfiction books for children and hopes to inspire others to share her passion by celebrating the creativity that can be found within the subject. Lou is also a photographer and avid wild swimmer. She lives in Bath, England, with her husband, fantasy novelist Joe Abercrombie, and their three children.

@LadyGrimdark
www.louabercrombie.com

LILIA MICELI

Lilia was born in Turin, Italy. When she was a little girl, she was always drawing and enjoyed turning words into images. This led her to study at the school of arts in Turin. Now Lilia is a professional illustrator. Her passion is dealing with important topics while also creating something beautiful. Lilia loves drawing all day long, but she also likes to share food and drinks with friends, to cuddle cute animals, and to pretend to be a mermaid.